CREATE

EXECUTE

REPEAT

by

Jordan Thomas

CreateSpace Publishing

South Carolina

2017

Table of Contents

This book is dedicated firstly to God, my family, friends, and those I've yet to meet during the rest of this journey called life.

With love, gratitude, and infinite blessings from the Lord above,

Jordan Thomas

Foreword by Jim Beach, international best-selling author and speaker:

The creativity you'll find in the book will have you engaged and inspire you to thrive in business. Jordan Thomas has inspired me to be, and become, great in many areas of my life because of his unique thinking. His artistic poetry and incredible singing abilities will inspire many to find their own greatness. I encourage you to read this book because many, like myself, find themselves struggling in business and we all can use creative thinking to turn things around. In chapters 4 & 7 you'll find what makes others creative and what it takes. We can learn from others just as the greatest minds have done to be successful. Learning from others mistakes, so that you don't repeat them, speeds up the results you hope to achieve -that's just one of the secrets to success! Make sure to highlight, take notes and apply all that you learn from this book. Be creative and have fun or your business will drive you crazy regardless of how successful your business runs. You'll be surprised how the tips you take away from this book can be used in the future. I'm confident that you'll enjoy what you read!

-Jim Beach -Mr Relentless International Personal Development Speaker, Author of The Nickname That Didn't Stick

Chapter 1: The Root of Your Fruit

It is very common in a society to have a tendency to infiltrate our God-given identities with manmade labels, especially if they do not seem nor attempt to understand another's point of view. Sometimes, we cannot seem to differentiate between correction and condemnation. Whenever we do not understand something, and growing up in a predominantly digital paradigm, we never question our own perception, our own behavior, our own misrepresentations, and notions that turn out to be false. It is always everyone around us but us. We have grown accustomed to shaming what we do not understand, and tightly gripping to our own perception and whenever it turns out to be falsehood, we continue to remain in denial. The ego plays a dominant role in this behavior. We witness it daily in various occasions, most recently, our current political season (this is as political as this book will get). With this into consideration, it is crucial to question everything around you, but also maintain respect. We have been taught that being skeptical is considered negative, especially if what we are being skeptical about is blindly accepted by the majority. If you do not question it or remain skeptical, you are bound to fall victim to falsehood.

In today's era of mainstream media, we are unfortunately very susceptible to it. This is why it ruins so many factors in life because we often forget to take time to discern with what we immerse ourselves in. If we discern and truly do so with a pure desire to further develop ourselves as people, and essentially, children of God, from there we'll learn to be watchful of the fruits we are given by those around us. We all have a desire to create something substantial and bigger than ourselves. As a start, we need to be cautious of the fruits we bear to ourselves and to others and make sure that they are fruits of the Holy Spirit. This especially applies to creating. If we fail to figure out why we put out the content we do, ultimately, it will all be in vain. Time is too vital and pressing for us to waste time and energy placing ourselves in circumstances that lack any significance or worth. I often wonder what type of fruit particular people are trying to bear based on the content I see them producing. In this context, the root equates to the source. Everything we put out into the world stems from a specific source and when that source is identified, that tells us whether we should bear this fruit the way we've been or change something about it within the process. What we create will reflect what lies within us in terms of values, beliefs, and the sentiments we're trying to express. As a society, new creations lead to satisfaction and in my personal opinion, we all deserve happiness in a way that aligns with God's will (not really deserve, it's all grace). We all are striving to be given the same opportunities, and evolve personally, mentally, and spiritually. What we often overlook is that the factor holding us back the most isn't always around us, it's not our boss, our co-workers, friends, or the mainstream media: it's *us*. We hold ourselves back in several ways: feeling sorry for ourselves, excessive pride, allowing ourselves to be defined by others, and simply accepting our own self-imposed limitations. We complain about things being too complacent or monotonous and the cruelty of the world, then we turn around and unknowingly (at times, knowingly) contribute to it. We are the reason that we provide more pain, bitterness, and anger to a world already with saturated hostility. What we as a society create will serve as a reflection of what we're about and what we feed ourselves with in terms of information, it reflects what we truly value as a society. This can either boost or hinder our creative flow and there is no in-between. The point of this read isn't to attempt to change any reader's way of thinking but to better enhance and leverage creativity, something God has given me a lot of to use in many areas of life thus far, and to apply it greatly in business and many facets of life. To make an analogy, we're all trees and the fruits we bear will indicate our performance in all that we pursue and engage in. These fruits are rooted in various contributions that we are to be weary of (not necessarily "positive" traits, but vital traits) including passion, consistency, originality, and a vision that will be made into effect by God's appointed time. Part of leveraging that creative side of us is delving not into the solution, but first at the problem at hand. Sometimes, we're so engulfed into wanting the solution but never delve deep into the problem with a full and clear awareness of it, other times we're quick to ramble about the problem at hand and without offering any solutions, otherwise known as being an armchair revolutionary. We're used to everything being instantaneous, but sometimes the fastest method of solving problems isn't always the most effective.

As recent as 2016, the average human attention span lasts only eight seconds, before it was twelve, coincidentally, due to smartphones. It's understandable that we have destinations to travel to, and priorities to finish as effectively as we can, but sometimes, the simplest thing people alike crave is the attention and consideration of others, especially those we are close to. Detail is an essential component in everything made. Even if it is something that we consider to be useless, like I stated previously, everything serves a specific purpose and once we get past the ego and seeking innovation based on our own needs, we will come to realize it contributes to something far greater than we could possibly ever comprehend. That is what separates the artist from any other profession. The artist sees many things others cannot, they interpret things from a base of emotion, feeling, and most visually prominent. Part of letting your creativity unleash is the type of emotion that will be communicated through the finished product. Due to this, you allow those around you to witness either something they resonate with or something that is new to them and can learn from. Whatever sentiment you display in the artistic process will show within the content itself. A joyful work of art will stem from a place of joy, a raw and transparent work of art will stem from a place of vulnerability and sensitivity. A poignant work of art will stem from a place of reflection, possibly anguish, and an intense sense of passion and catharsis. Not only is it important for one to distinguish and discern their fruits but the source as well, for both are equally important. Everyone has to start something from somewhere, but not necessarily from simply anywhere. This is where discernment comes in. Take time to evaluate all of your surroundings and who you surround yourself with. Surround yourself with encouragers, givers, believers, creators, executors of ideas bigger than them, and those that are positive but honest. Always maintain awareness. It is awareness that is displayed in whatever you create, as well as your intentions. Ask yourself what your intentions are. This is what I mean by the root of your fruit, the motives and intentions of what you create. These are crucial and even when you think people can't see or notice them, they can. Creativity starts also with imagination and bringing mental representations. These are the driving forces of anything we set our minds to and ultimately show why we do what it is that we do with no frills whatsoever. Not everyone will appreciate what God has given to you, that's why He gave it to you and only you. Everyone is not going to understand nor have the decency to want to understand your vision, journey, and grind, but it's not for you to simply waste away. For creative types especially, it is important to know that while God has blessed us with individual gifts and talents, the fruit we produce with those talents is what it all boils down to. You will know how you are using your gift by what you yield. This has been proven time and time again as a mean to suppress art and reduce its significance to sheer wickedness and a lifestyle of pretentious luxury and immorality. Then again, in the midst of our conception, we were all given free will, and surely, those promoting and perpetuating this type of living are aware of the consequences. A person can possess all of the talent that can possibly be stored in only one human, but if the fruits they are bearing are not of the Holy Spirit such as faith, joy, love, and goodness, then no matter how much that gift is skilled and crafted to their definition of perfection, then it ultimately means nothing.

Chapter 2: Progress, Not Perfection

Growing up, we have all been led to believe that what society believes to be perfection is what we all should live up to, and if not, we're unfortunately perceived as failures or good-for-nothings. These expectations range from physical appearance, style of clothing, and personal preferences based on one's generation or environment. The world's perception of perfection has resorted to some of the most unnecessary tasks expected to be done include body image, plastic surgery, and behaving in a certain way. Often, that behavior is rooted in what the world wants you to be, but not what God wants you to be. There are many distractions in the world with a sole purpose to corrupt and infiltrate our minds along with the creativity and expressions that lies within them. These distractions are bereft of substance and are designed only to serve our flesh. What one feeds the flesh will be temporary, but what is fed to the soul will nourish it and endure forever. Truthfully, and as a Christian, the only state of perfection is that of Christ, and we all fall short.

For those that have been pressing on and trying daily to live up to what society deems as perfect, the truth is that it won't happen and personally, that's perfectly fine. We don't have to keep superficially editing ourselves by some of the so-called standards. Ultimately, no matter how much one attains that is considered perfection by many, there will always be progress required. Within the development of this continuous progress, there will be people who may try to suppress that growth or downsize it. God did not give them what He gave you so clearly, some would misunderstand it to begin with. When encountering people throughout life, early on, you must learn the difference between being liked versus being respect. Respect is much more valuable, enduring, and necessary than being liked. To be liked sometimes causes people to go against who they were made to be, trying to become what others expect of them. When it constantly occurs, eventually, it will end up happening so much, you will begin to lose sight of who you truly and authentically are. This is the joy of being creative and leveraging that creativity: I firmly believe people do their absolute best when they are not attempting to please those around them, because they are simply going for what God has called them to individually do, and that alone is better than any form of imitation.

As a society, we are too consumed with trying to increase our social status and embellish our outer layers while our inner layers remain lifeless and stunted. It must start within the mind and developing not a mindset of perfection, but one of continuous progress and development. For artists and creators, it can be quite pressuring within the midst of that follow-up to a great start and even as a starter. Every creation is different from the other in some way. The key is not conformity, but consistency and there is a difference. You will be able to remain consistent in your craft with reliance on God to be innovative and add diversity and variety.

I still recall various times in my life during the past year as a freshman in college where I stressed myself out because of an obligation to reach an illusion of perfection, whether that was becoming the "perfect" college student, whatever that may mean (ivy league, 4.0). I am not saying that this was not impossible for me, however and admittedly, I am definitely not the best example. All my life, I have seen those who stress perfection, and refer that to what is ultimately far from it. There is a difference between perfection and excellence. We're into numbers, whether it is the number of social media followers, likes, retweets, or college degrees (i.e "If I can attain this certain number of that certain object, life will be great). Measuring our results by comparing is truly a disaster in the making. We may get what we hope for in the end, but never forget the amount of pain, backlash, suffering, fighting, and ridicule some have to endure to get it. Perfection may not be attainable, but excellence is and can be through relentless faith through Christ and acting on that faith, setting reasonable goals, and aligning your motives, intentions, thoughts, and actions with all that is in God's will, plan, and purpose for your life. When you strive for perfection, you will ultimately fall short and end up constantly comparing yourself to those you are trying to become. Becoming who the world wants you to be would be an insult to your own soul, your family, and true friends, and mostly to God. He made you in His own individual plan and image and to abandon that would be an absolute waste. When you strive for excellence, you are focused on doing the right thing, without approval of the world around you or receiving recognition. Aiming for perfection includes setting goals that are nearly impossible, while those that pursue excellence rest easy knowing they've gone as far as God has allowed them to.

One of the key differences between perfection and excellence is progress. Perfection seekers won't value progress because they personally seem to be set and fully skilled in everything in their lives, but pursuers of excellence always acknowledge that there will always be progress and that there is no final destination in their craft, unless it is stopped by death. Means of perfection have been crafted several times throughout our society and if we don't reach it, we're made to feel that as humans, we lack worth. That's the difference between pleasing the world and pleasing God. He does not demand perfection, and if so, then I guarantee it would not be measured by anything of carnality or material. God's perfection does not align with human or societal perfection, the difference is that one's relationship with Him supersedes anything and everything of human life. In contrast to what some say, striving for perfection does not require one to collect objects, equate your goals with that of the norm, or act as if you never make mistakes. Part of striving for excellence includes acknowledging that you are bound to make mistakes but attaining the wisdom to not repeat those same ones. Different mistakes are inevitable and are needed for growth, but the same ones occurring constantly are worthless. The goal of perfection is not to be made into a trophy to be displayed, but to be used as a vessel and to have God continue to take you where He intends for you to go.

As creative people, we know this firsthand that mistakes are bound to occur. That is simply part of the creative, or artistic process, whatever you'd like to call it. Mistakes equal growth and that growth is the key component to always make sure you're innovating instead of staying in the same routine. In an increasingly ego-driven society with a tendency to deem what we see on television perfection (though a majority of it is falsehood), we are shown a display of what seems effortless as an attempt to make what is actually challenging look easy. This is definitely not the case. Part of leveraging one's creativity and striving for excellence instead of perfection means to abandon the need to always be right. The problem is whenever one constantly has the need to prove themselves right and others wrong is the lack of humility and the lack of a bigger and clearer understanding. One never stops learning no matter what stage of life they are at. Skills must continue to be developed. There are many personality traits that require creativity that we probably never took time to look at.

As it is stated in Exodus 35:30-33 in the Bible, particular artists and people of craft were filled with the spirit of God, skill, intelligence, knowledge, and craftsmanship. When you gain these abilities, God wants and expects you to share them with others, like all other gifts. He wants you not to neglect them, but to work on it and improve it to share it with those around you rather than hoarding it for one's own personal gain. Here on earth, perfection is not required, because no matter what you do, there will always be resistance, opposition, and ridicule from a considerable amount. Let your craft and ideas stem from the heart, and genuine instead of forced. And in conclusion for this segment, aim for progress, not perfection.

Chapter 3: The Miseducation of Confidence

For someone to increase and continually use their sense of being creative, it's best to start in their youth. Creativity's one of the main ingredients to success, and it's a shame for it to sometimes be frowned upon. Perhaps this could be because a creative idea could shatter societal norms and what's socially expected. Early on, the mind of a child is curious, spontaneous, and eager to explore. It gives one a voice and the ability to express their thoughts in some of the most diverse ways from writing to business development. Some may disagree with the following but I believe schools are suppressing the individuality and creativity students possess. Teaching is supposed to come from a place of passion and enthusiasm, not monotony and social/intellectual docility. The key to an effective job well done in this case is engagement. Children are naturally curious and creative, engaging in activities that stimulate wonder and exhilaration. In these years, we've been taught to never question things that ought to be questionable, to go with the flow, to simply let things be and to not change things too drastically only because they are not ready to handle innovation. Creativity is not an exam that one has to pass or fail, and even if you were to fail which is highly and logically impossible, it's not the end of the world.

Personally, part of the reason our public schools are losing creativity is because students are too fearful of ever daring to question what occurs regularly, especially if what they are being fed serves no eternal or significant purpose. Could it stem from a lack of confidence? Most likely. What parents tell and pass down to their children will serve as a catalyst for what they pass down to others. Though I am not a parent yet, growing up, one of the biggest lessons my father, Hiram has taught me was to have confidence and assurance in myself. I like to take it a step further and seek God who gives me all that I need to live and sustain, and call it "Godfidence", as some put it via social media. The main difference between biblically based confidence and materially based confidence is that confidence that is biblically based won't come from a place of pride and arrogance, but will still allow you to achieve your goals in the name of the Holy Spirit. Growing up, we are told that it's best to pursue subjects such as mathematics, science, business, and law (there is nothing wrong with these subjects). Pursuing an art to some is a waste of money, value, and time, but I beg to differ, if used and applied in a good and reasonable way.

There are many ways to implement and maintain creativity in public schools such as various long-term projects. These projects will give students a chance to work on a project with no deadlines, as sometimes deadlines tend to stand in the way of fully branching out and exploring. Students love to figure things out and sometimes the most effective ways of doing so don't stem from a book. In no way am I advocating for students or children in general to go after things with no help or direction. Offer reasonable points and guide them, but don't control them. One of the key elements that make up a child and its future is influence. Children are shaped by what is instilled in them by their parents and what they're displayed, with that said, they will grow up believing what it is you tell them. When children are given the gift of creativity, they must learn to retain it and nourish it throughout life without having others try to taint it. One of the ways I've retained my sense of creativity growing up was keeping a journal. Growing up, it was almost being the daily writer and artist in the family, constantly buying notebooks and writing anything and everything that came to mind, from songs to kanji symbols to various drawings and sketches. Most people get through the day using written routines. Through the years, I've attempted to do this, but it personally didn't work for me (There's irony to this considering how much I write on a daily basis). When it comes to free time, I prefer spontaneity. With spontaneity that's ultimately purposeful, there's more of an effective outcome. When people go to practice whether it's an instrument, or painting, we tend to worry if we won't be as productive as we'd like to. In this moment, anxiety begins to infiltrate, and from there, once the anxiety increases, our ideas come to a sudden halt, and suddenly, we stop creating. All of this coincides with the theme of this chapter, which is confidence. Whenever we're in the midst of creating, there is always a bit of doubt, but in the beginning, it's common to invalidate our own ideas usually due to concern of what others think. Spontaneity in the creative process doesn't ruin it, it is instead a must. It means performing tasks and actions without really (over) thinking, or doing without taking time to analyze it. It's about allowing every idea and concept developed in your mind to flow and be drawn out. Once this is all done and all ideas are finally poured out, then you'll have the time to begin editing and revising.

There's a thin line between confidence and arrogance. Part of having creative confidence is knowing there is much more for one to learn along their journey. You should never get to the point that you're an independent creative overall genius, because even geniuses humble themselves and seek help. Establishing it signifies that God's given you the type of confidence you're unable to find within the things of the world such as clothes, cars, or other earthly luxuries. Rather than those stated, creative confidence in Christ means fully knowing your strengths, weaknesses, not allowing your weaknesses to succumb yourself or your craft, and daring to be innovative when the world goes against it. This type of confidence will allow you to fully exercise your right to be eclectic, innovative, and mostly, original. It will allow you to do more than you will ever expect, and go as far as God intends. We have been led to believe that copying is a more effective route and while that is an advancement towards the human flesh, it does nothing to ultimately nourish the spirit, nor advance us toward fulfilling what we were called to do. Everything we ever achieve in this lifetime should stem from all that God has placed in us and nothing outside of that. It is foolish to take sole credit in things we ultimately don't deserve. Doing so, these achievements will be worthless. Confidence in the world may get you far but confidence in Christ will carry you for miles upon miles.

Chapter 4: Same People, Different Habits

This book is not designed at all to put creative people on pedestals, but it is measured in some parts to display what sets them apart from other types of people. To describe a creative person, the majority of people would possibly say, "rebellious", "independent", or having an unusual mindset. The truth is there is no definitive way to completely identify a creative person. Of all the labels the world tends to throw out such as those mentioned, perhaps the biggest factor they all have in common is that God has given them the ability to think for themselves without being influenced by elements of society or the world. That ability to think for one's self extends beyond art, such as in social and political situations. Thinking for yourself is a sign of strength, a weakness would be to allow something or someone else to determine your views and opinions on matters of any kind. If you go through life just accepting and believing literally every single thing anyone tells you, you're bound for a life of manipulation and folly. The Lord we serve is too I pity those who constantly feel that they have to fit into a particular box. All they are doing when trying to fit into one is abandon their self-worth. That self-worth will begin to be validated by societal opinions. Trying to fit in is never worth dying over, physically or spiritually.

Creative people usually have a vast amount of interests, instead of boxing themselves in with only one. That's the essence of creativity itself. However, having so many interests can be a bit of a distraction especially if they don't serve a purpose or if we are trapped in uncertainty. For examples, my interests include music, books, writing, art, photography, tea, and many more. Having a niche is fine, especially if you're in the field of marketing. Those who thrive on creativity have many interests and passions throughout life. There is an unlimited amount of curiosity when dwelling within a complicated world. Some people never stop learning and they constantly ask questions. Some of these questions may not be the most helpful in certain situations, but if they don't get asked, how else will they be addressed? For us, there is no specific time that we're scheduled to ask or figure something out.

Creative people have a tendency to be more productive than busy. Growing up, we've all been aware of the need to always be busy, and anything short of that equates to laziness. I prefer to be productive. From what I've witnessed, most of those that see themselves as busy usually get little to nothing done. Very few people I know are truly busy and it shows, but they always make time for what matters to them. One of my favorite authors and inspirations for the subject of creativity, Mark McGuinness, stated something of this nature to be called a creative generalist.

A creative generalist is someone who are at their most comfortable or most creative when engaging in different projects all at once. Some generalists are comfortable doing several projects at once, while others may want to restrict themselves to only a few, either way is fine. Another term of his is known as a "whirling devish", which I personally identify with. This is someone who has many creative careers and interests that go intertwine with one another. In our increasingly busy and rush hour-like society where time flies at a rapid rate, we still get to our location whether it's work, home, or school.

While we may appear to be confident in our steps and where we think we're heading, in a way, we truly have no idea where we're going and that's not only in the physical sense. Because me and others I've come across prefer to be productive rather than busy, we allow others to see that we apply clarity before applying action. Going straight into action without certainty can lead to consequences. And you can't lead into action without a plan.

There are those that like to tell us how busy they are because it may help their ego or worldly status. For those who are productive, they allow the results of their work to do the talking. Being busy doesn't help one's creative flow, because when you're busy, you're allowing yourself to become occupied with other things that hinder your opportunity to be creative. In an ever-growing professional realm of the world, we are obsessed with taking into consideration a particular email, a particular text message, TV episode, or other task at a particular moment. In doing so, our focus is on getting each task done one by one and moving on to the next one, rather than focusing on one task at a time and its individual value. At this point, trying to cram it all into extra time is futile. When one is extremely busy, they are so consumed into what is to be done today that they never allow themselves to explore what else is possible that can affect them positively in the future. Being creative doesn't require having all the answers nor does it equate to doing activities such as yoga in order to have it. It starts with putting it into your mind first and learning to think creatively. It's not necessarily the answer to solving problems, but instead an essential way of thinking that can lead to better ways at solving problems.

The creative types tend to get immersed in their own vulnerability. This is an important step in a society made to hide our pain. Pure emotion is the key component to a lot of art throughout the course of planet Earth. Vulnerability is not about displaying your emotions openly so that others may see and sympathize. It is to be in solitude and allow those emotions and sentiments to be drawn and poured out, allowing those who witness it an invitation into what you have experienced without being too naïve to let them have control of your soul. A better word for this would be catharsis. Creative people know when they are wrong and they are not afraid to admit it. 80% of people defend themselves to avoid admitting they are wrong. This is why more humility is needed especially in leadership, real leaders display it in any encounter. They are humble and have a willingness to change their minds when previous decisions didn't seem right or correct. Mistakes as a leader are meant to serve as lessons rather than catalysts for rash judgment. By seeking new ideas and new directions from their peers, they instill more growth within that company and its values, especially in an industry as complex as that of business. Constant change is vital to the creative side of anyone. The moment we stop evolving will be the day that what we produce is dead. Creativity has no starting nor ending time. There's a quote on social media stating that our creative peak usually arrives between the hours of 2-3 a.m. On the contrary, it can strike during any time of the day and at any stage in life, not just in our youth. It is not exclusive to highly artistic people. It is available to everyone, some just use it more. Creative people are serious risk takers, and we are not afraid to create the unexpected, the unheard of, and the possibility of ridicule, judgment, and criticism not only from those around them, but also themselves. They know exactly what it is that they want and they are not afraid to go after it, no matter what may stand in their way. It is important to take the risks not from a place of fear, because that will end up being displayed by self-imposed doubt and limitations. Take risks from a purpose of not wanting to compromise your vision will result in a much better aftermath. Whatever you leave out in your creation will eventually find itself onto your next body of work.

Another misconception is that people are their most creative when they are happy. There is very little evidence that links creativity with increased happiness. From experience, I am at my most creative when I'm in anguish, distress, frustration, confusion, and when I allow God to speak to me whenever I either have nothing to say or feel that shouldn't say anything. The beginning may sound odd, because most people view getting into their creative zone when they are happy and full of enthusiasm. Creativity can develop in any emotion one feels at a certain moment. Sometimes the creative types are mistaken as being loners but along with other professions, being in solitude has its benefits and can help us generate more, if not, better ideas. Most of us are ready to create and contribute to something to the world and leave a mark while we are still alive, even in the midst of blockage and obstructions. Sometimes, the biggest obstructions are ourselves, repressing ourselves and returning ourselves back to a reductive paradigm. I must admit that sometimes, it's hard to get into my creative zone due to the busyness of the world, as well as personal and social responsibilities. But at the end of the day, it's important to take time out for self-care. Self-care is not selfish, some of us just tend to make it selfish. This type of productivity is what aligns with excellence as discussed in Chapter 2. It's better to create a single, enriching, and vivacious piece of content rather than twenty pieces of mediocrity.

In any type of professional or corporate environment, you are bound to deal with matters that bring stress and pressure. As all of us tend to relieve work and job stress differently, it is easy for us to become discouraged. One of the many reasons behind this temporary discouragement is because our focus is placed on the wrong matter. Instead of resorting to feelings of helplessness and despair in the midst of situations that require a high-level of detail and attentiveness, we ought to focus on the ability to impact and better the lives of those who we are serving. It is vital to find joy in the midst of pressure, purpose in the midst of apathy, and clarity in the midst of confusion. All of these become intertwined once we get to the reality that our endeavors are not about us but about God and the people He places in our lives. This brings true joy in the midst of pressuring and overwhelming situations. Once we seek this mindset and what creates long-lasting joy not just in business but in any endeavor, then we will possess a greater and continuously growing love and passion for our craft. As a future educator and professor, I hope with God as my eternal guide that I will be able to create and continuously cultivate a learning environment that is creative, innovative, and ultimately impactful. One of the biggest misconceptions we have about creativity is that it is limited only to the arts. By limiting it only to this, we stifle the creative potential that lies within people of many diverse fields including education, marketing, ministry, etc. Creativity can be sought anywhere but it should not be sought everywhere, especially at the expense of your soul. To thrive creatively does not require gimmicks of any kind. It includes a powerful mixture of collaboration, humility, a willingness to grow by making mistakes and constant discomfort. Thriving creatively doesn't occur when a creation is complete, it occurs when the creation serves a bigger purpose than its creator.

Chapter 5: Innovation in Business

In the business world, no matter how exceptional one may believe their product or contribution to it to be, if you lack the ability to innovate, you are bound to be left behind in the marketplace. We are in a very competitive marketplace and innovation is what maintains any business, helps it thrive and become successful. This is the ultimate driving force: the ability to pitch and execute new ideas, products, and services that are effective and aligned with what is demanded by your targeted audience. There may be some things customers want but do not fully realize yet, in this case, there must always be awareness. It is easier to acknowledge a creative idea than to implement it. One revolutionary idea can change the entire core of your company.

With innovation must first come failure and the willingness to fail. Amazon founder, Jeff Bezos stated regarding this: "Failure and innovation are inseparable twins". If I were to have my own business, for example, a soon-to-be clothing line starting out, and if I failed the first few attempts within the development of this venture, I would honestly be completely fine with it. I might seem crazy or average-minded upon admitting that, but the truth is that failure is included in the process, though we did not sign up for it in particular. Those going into business or starting out, if you are not willing to fail and make mistakes throughout the beginning stages, then unfortunately, it might not be right for you. That is the reason for the existence of resilience, when failure occurs, then either what you are trying to pursue isn't what God had in store for you or there is something in it that you are doing wrong and haven't realized yet. Failure leads you to new business ideas and methods you didn't know you had, further igniting your creativity. Therefore, failure is needed, but sometimes, we take advantage of this and end up confining ourselves to a prison of conformity called mediocrity. Mediocrity is like a personification of Satan telling you to give up on God's plan for you. It will do whatever it can to make you complacent, docile, and comfortable with achieving the same results in the exact same format over and over again, knowing there can be improvement. You will never know what it is that your customers and consumers want unless you listen and engage with them. Engagement is the key to maintaining long-lasting, professional, and effective relationships.

A problem currently in the business world, online and off, is the lack of engagement. Because of the lack of engagement, it equals various consequences such as a new set of team members and associates, a lack of productivity from your current workers, and a lack of motivation, reason, or purpose to do their job. In the business world, engagement with workers is so much more than simply giving orders and reiterating particular points. You have to be willing to be transparent with them, serving them, addressing any concerns especially that could potentially affect the entire company, and doing what you can for them to perform the tasks in their job effectively and to the best of their ability. Whenever you engage and whomever you engage with, leave your ego at home. Ask questions, the kind of questions that challenge your mindset as well as the mindsets of everyone around you including what can they change about their business that is potentially causing harm, or are they completely aligned on their focus or on a different agenda. These questions will not only instill growth but they will draw you and your team closer to true innovation instead of regurgitating the same concepts. In this case, a leader might ask his or herself:

- Do they value creativity as much as they say they do, and if not, how can they implement it more effectively?

- Do they set an example of what they want to seek from the creative realm of business?

While in general, creativity is mostly unstructured, in the business world, there must be structure. It is not merely about your own creativity as a leader, but mostly about the creativity of your team. In order to bring this out, you have to be willing to trust your fellow team members with different ideas and allow them to try not just with your help, but eventually on their own. Simon Sinek said it best: "A team is not a group of people that work together. A team is a group of people that trust each other". Innovation will not only promote one's business but it'll add more value to the purpose of that business and allow you to view the business's values and possible future opportunities from a different perspective. Innovation in business will not only allow you to create more loyalty towards your current target audience but also generate and attract new ones as well without compromising you or your business's core values.

The most common type of innovation businesses apply is disruptive innovation. This kind includes a network or market disrupting an already existing network with new products and affiliations. They start from the bottom and work their way up to eventually overthrow their competitors. From this stemmed creative disruption which includes disrupting an existing market with a strikingly creative message. Disruption, in this case, is deviating from whatever the norm of what the business at hand tends to be, it ceases any form of mediocrity possible. Exceptional influencers of business and marketing include those that have the boldness and "Godfidence" to shatter the already existing standards placed on them by average and limited mindsets. We have all had fixed limitations based on our own strengths. When you acknowledge that you are not capable of everything using false confidence and instead let God intervene, this is where real change begins to manifest itself onto what is being pursued (Faith it till you make it). This alludes to Chapter 3. Without confidence, in the business world, you won't aim too far. Faking it can only do so much, especially in this realm. Little things can sometimes stop us from being confident in ourselves business-wise, such as a product thought of as not being good enough, or a particular way of spreading one's message. We're sometimes hindered by the opinions and thoughts of others, and even when we think it doesn't impact us, they do.

Confidence may be the most important factor entering into business. It creates an enduring impact on how you do your job, how you manage your employees, or if you are an employee, how you motivate your fellow team members. It produces the outcome of whether or not you attain what you consider success. It's definitely not something you are born with, and instead something that must continue to be developed over time. Some of the reasons businesspeople lack confidence is because they create incredibly high expectations, they might be too hard on themselves, they could be having an off-day or longer period of time or they most likely are not producing the results they would like. The results that come out are based on how much we put in to begin with. If our effort is halfway, then our results will be the same. Being the loudest and brashest one in the room is not required starting in business. This produces false confidence, and no matter how real it may seem, people will realize that it is fake while denial plays its role. A creative leader knows how to be convicting, starting with themselves. Creative conviction starts with yourself instead of seeking external approval. It starts with possessing the need to bring something new, fresh, and exciting into the industry you are in.

As a boss, in order to utilize creativity and leverage innovation in your business, you have to be humble enough to understand that you don't contain all of the answers. Don't magnify the weaknesses of your employees when you hired them based on their strengths, but still give criticism that is constructive and helpful, not hurtful and ego-boosting. There is nothing wrong with allowing your employees to voice personal input to matters that concern business aspects that ought to be improved. Sometimes, lessons of humility end up being sought out and a worker might know something the boss does not that could end up benefitting him and his team. Many business leaders are said to have not used creativity because past ideas seemed nearly impossible or it may seem like a waste of time. Exploring and applying creative strategies that align with the goals of a business is never a waste of time. It is an extremely important factor in business and the workplace and can make a difference in producing end results as well as the business's environment overall. Once they are implemented, the road to vital and creative disruption is closer.

To apply creativity in a stagnant workplace means to come up with multiple unique strategies that have never been used before rather than using only one. It means applying what is considered out of the ordinary and merging team members' views and personal perspectives that are benefitting to the business and task at hand. However, do not get too comfortable with current ideas, because even those could change eventually and they do due to everchanging customs and demands from forthcoming consumers. This is where reevaluation comes in. Reevaluate what is used creatively for your business so that it could either be used again, differently, or never again. Being in a fast-paced job field, business ideas can change relentlessly without any warning. Handle these rapid changes with dignity and an appropriate response. In this realm, an appropriate response would be to accept the changes and develop a positive mindset focused on what could go right instead of what could go wrong. If the changes don't sit well with you, in this case, an appropriate response would be to share your concern with your boss. If you are not comfortable with this, feel free to voice your concern to your peers. What doesn't change in the marketplace maintains a lack of growth. Customers are attracted by freshness and variety in business instead of rehashing the same of everything. It is crucial to stay innovative in a world dominated by machines. Possibly in the future, machines could end up doing what us humans have been doing but better than we ever did. Hopefully, this won't occur too soon. Whenever someone questions the idea of innovation for their company, keep in mind that it is better to have a variety of creative ideas and have that business thrive than to apply regurgitated strategies and have it fail.

Chapter 6: For The Artists

This specific chapter is for artists of all types: musicians, writers, painters, poets, photographers, even those that apply art into their everyday life. As an artist, our purpose for what we do is to share with the world our most deepest, expressive, passionate, and visually communicative displays, works, and pieces of content. While doing so, we need to fully exercise our God-given ability to create. We need to always possess the power of the Holy Spirit and allow it to work through and within us so that we know what we produce reflects God, His fruits, and the values of Christianity. What we produce ought to be beneficial for those around us. When we know that what we are putting out there is helping others in a positive way, I believe that is when we know that God is using us to make sustainable impacts. Every type of art can be used to benefit the world.

Musicians constantly work on the craft of either their voice or instruments. It takes long and tedious processes and hours full of shaping and expanding that craft and seeing more and more that we are capable of doing with it. There is so much more to being a musician than recording albums, global tours, talk shows, and TV performances. Like the iceberg model, there is a lot of dedication, practice, moments where we feel like giving up, and a lot of enticements in a treacherous music industry especially if one is not careful. It takes a lot for us to pursue our craft the way it is intended without any compromise or worldly influence.

Writers possess the ability to use the utensil of their choice to pour their heart out and let their sentiments overflow onto paper like a great lake. A true writer never has to restrain their ideas for the sake of pleasing those around them and has no problem expressing their truth, no matter how others may feel about it. Every writer starts out with a first draft and not being pleased with it. Whether it's nonfiction, poetry, or something philosophical, the pen of a writer is like a sword with the ability to pierce through paper and retrieving parts of themselves that have now been poured out.

Painters contribute to far more than art galleries and a painting can sometimes depict more than a human could at a certain moment. Contemporary works evoke alike sentiments regarding historical events such as 9/11, The Civil Rights Movement, and issues involving race, power, and global political tension. Every color evokes a different meaning and expression. Poets, like writers, express by writing and sometimes reciting. Not every poem may rhyme but also every poem might not be clear in the beginning. The essence of poetry is not crystal clear but it also isn't enigmatic either. Artists are not artists because of the possibility of worldwide fame or monetary riches. They are artists because God has placed in them the ability to move and enrich the hearts and souls of thousands (or millions) with lush, captivating works they have devoted so much time into creating. They are artists because they refuse to let the world influence them to exchange their authenticity for imitation. As artists, we really need to recognize and appreciate the value and time we put into our work. If not, then no one else will either. Various works convey different emotions but all derive from the blood, sweat, and tears being poured out onto every little contribution that makes the work in its complete form. There is constant artistic thriving and growth and a shift in every individual progression, and personally, the biggest components that help are the work of God and the ability to persevere. Perseverance and passion are what makes a true artist who they are, the ability to persist in the midst of a society with those who want to compromise art for the sake of personal or monetary gain and suppress those who speak out against and confront the still-occurring injustices. Growing up as an artist, and from what I've learned, artists musts do what is necessary to maintain their artistic integrity and sense of authenticity. It is easier to lose than to regain it. We were not conceived to be controlled, manipulated, or boxed in by manmade labels and societal constructs. I believe an artist's sole purpose is to constantly go against the grain and in the process, create things that are ultimately bigger than themselves. The point of creating art is to share it with everyone so that they may receive something beneficial and an invite to what God has implemented inside of us.

For artists who constantly feel discouraged by those around them and those who are too hard on themselves, please know that you are not alone. In the artistic process, we have tendencies to discourage ourselves and boggle our minds with negativity and criticism that radiates a be-all-and-end-all sentiment. We end up having to compare ourselves to others, specifically famous individuals. For artists who find themselves always placing limits upon their craft for the sake of trying to please people, ultimately, you're doing what God has called you to do whether or not others are affected by it. There are people who will find an issue in literally everything you put your mind to. Let them, how they perceive you is none of your business. In a world where you are able to create anything and execute that, create what is revolutionary, beneficial, and an enhancement in your field, creative flow, artistic process, and life overall. Learn from others and study from those who have done what you aspire to do. Life is always going to become overwhelmingly busy, sometimes beyond our control. The key is not completely giving up your crafts, it is balance and learning to incorporate that craft while dealing with the unexpected turns and twists within the realities of everyday living in this world. The strengths that come are to be incorporated into your character. Utilize the strengths that come with being an artist to manage and maintain a life you won't have to compromise yourself for. Whatever you do for your day-to-day job, don't let it kill you if it involves factors you don't enjoy. It is part of the process, and not every part of it will be based on one's personal liking. We may not be responsible for what life may throw at us, but we are always responsible for how we allow it to change us, whether it's for better or for worse. A way to retain your creativity that I have done all my life is keep a notebook or journal. The experience of writing is a lot different using paper or a notebook rather than a mobile device, and better I might add. An artist must stop trying to create themselves as someone else's perception of perfection. No matter how hard you try, the other party will always try to nitpick, pick you apart, and find something new every day to scrutinize. While I believe everyone has the ability to tap into their creative flow, some unfortunately prefer to do it in the way that is quicker.

Being in an instantaneous society, the problem with that is that you will never truly delve and explore into all that you are capable of doing. Creativity requires a lot of patience, the patience to think, feel, be uncomfortable, learn from someone else's pace and perspective and fail repeatedly. Perhaps one of the biggest ways to retain it would be to surround yourself more with creative people, and learn from them as well as collaborate. Be sure to turn off distractions as well, especially in a generation where our mobile phones have reached the same level of importance as air in our lungs. While it has its perks and many benefits, they can definitely be detrimental. Turn them off every once in a while. Being sedentary will never lead to more creativity and artistic growth. In any piece of work you may be working on, talk about it, and be constructive about it. Talk about what you aspire to do with the work, and the steps you will have to take, write it down if you need to. Prayer is a must as well. If you are seeking more creative energy and motivation, and if you can't seem to find it anywhere in the world, you know you will find it in the Lord, for He is the creator of all things and the most creative force imaginable. We were not called to blend in with the mundaneness and monotony of societal norms, if we are to live and exist in a way of Christ, we ought to do it not only creatively but boldly and courageously. While the Gospel is black and white in essence, and nothing but, we are able to serve Christ in a way that is multicolored. More of this will be in detail in the next chapter.

Chapter 7: The Three C's

Living a creative life involves a lot in the process as all of us already know. So far, in my creative journey, which I will elaborate in more detail later on in this book, I've utilized and leveraged many core components to maintain my sense of creativity. Some worked better than others but they are all important components to possess. It was a challenge to narrow them down but I decided to provide to readers three key components that have helped me the most and that I believe are beneficial to one's sense of creativity: consistency, change, and Christ:

We all know the creative process can be rough and uneasy but whenever creativity merges with business, specifically marketing, the key is consistency. Merging the two together can help your business, brand, or both be more recognizable in the midst of any confusion. Visual elements and signs have become extremely successful and creative marketing tactics that have maintained its business for years. For example, the M in the "McDonald's" sign instantly stands out due to its shape and size, and sits atop and in the middle of the actual name, as well as Pop Tarts featuring an arched and semi-dynamic type logo for its brand. By learning these types of examples and incorporating creativity into your brand as often as possible, you will then be able to establish your business's identity and have created its own place in the world of business. The best types of creative messages are the ones that attract not just support, but also longstanding loyalty from consumers. Consistency in creativity is just as important in life overall as it is in business. To remain consistent through it all, stay confident as previously discussed and never lose your passion and desire to create simply because of mere rejection. Like I've stated before, we are bound to feel frustration, anger, and confusion in our creative process. Let that stem from a place of wanting to do better and improve instead of a place of wanting to compete with anyone.

Change is a must in this process hence why a business is supposed to thrive. To apply this, you must have a deep insight and understanding within your industry of where you are bound to go. Industries are constantly changing, sometimes radically. Understanding changes in your business means refusing to adapt to current trends of your competitors, shutting out any temptations, and really analyzing how you are doing business so you will know what needs to be changed and what does not need to be changed. Handle these changes with tactfulness and respect, because they could possibly be made due to many circumstances, most likely ever-changing demands of customers and consumers. Of course, all changes are meant to be effective for each business but going through and delving into the importance of change will help understand which of them will be necessary. Be wary of changes that could potentially damage the company in any way either by its most important values or assets.

The last key here and undoubtedly most important is Christ who will provide to you more than you will ever need even when it seems like the least possibility. Seeking creativity in Christ will never leave you feeling unmoved or uninspired. Art does not have to be separated from one's faith in order for it to be successful, as opposed to what is said. As Christians, we have the opportunity to manifest what God places into our hearts, minds, and souls onto many platforms like paper, a canvas, or a microphone and glorify Him. Plus, in my personal opinion, creativity is a must as a church and body in Christ. We are used to seeing the same topics of sermons, the same worship songs with the same beats and tempos. While the message overall is what matters most, there is a point in all of this. If everything remains the same, then that sense of passion surely is lacking. Creativity is a part of our faith simply because we were made by a creative God. It is important that we continually discern in this process. What we may think has good intentions can turn out to be the exact opposite, especially in this case. An artist in Christ does not have to adjust their faith to the world's preference nor does it have to be overly preachy. What we do with our art is to have it provide truth, healing, and spiritual awareness of the magnificence that is our Lord and savior. We ought to seek God to create something truly magnificent in His eyes that will truly shock and spiritually rouse the world. His creativity is not reduced only to things of nature such as rainbows or sunsets.

When God created the universe, he used His word like a writer uses their pen or pencil. We are living, breathing instruments made by the

Divine Creator of all things. God's creativity is forever enduring and learning from it can generate some of the most exquisite and incredible creations that we probably cannot pull off without Him. It will expand beyond church services and enter deep within our hearts and minds in the midst of transformation, for only He is capable of doing so. When we truly explore, we will surely be mesmerized as His creative power shows more and more as time goes by.

Chapter 8: My Creative Journey

Throughout my twenty years of living thus far, if there is one thing I am grateful for that God has given me, aside from the gifts of life and discernment, it is the gift of creativity. It has truly been something that has allowed me to challenge myself over and over again, to explore new possibilities, and expand on it. My creative journey began at the age of 5. I had many remedies to boost my creativity, mostly prayer, immersing in silence or nature, or certain foods such as tea. Growing up, music was, I believed and still do today, my ultimate calling in life. I am grateful that I grew up surrounded by music with passion, effort, musicality, and most of all, wisdom. I did not pursue the craft of music until the age of 8. My twin brother, Drew and I had been undeservingly blessed by the Lord above with the ability to demonstrate musical skills including singing, dancing, songwriting, piano and guitar. During this point, our main components were singing and songwriting. We had a very diverse musical upbringing, ranging from gospel, pop, R& B, soul, dance, jazz, hip hop, disco, Latin, and more. Growing up, being incorporated was the importance of artistic expansion and branching out. Branching out in this case was the key to escaping our comfort zones. The difference is that branching out with God's help will not mislead you while branching out and falling into just any path can be quite perilous.

Growing up with a Christ-filled upbringing, it was crucial for Drew and I as musicians to remain careful and aware of the motives and agendas of such earthly entities and protect our God-given spiritual gifts. There were moments of compromise but fortunately, they did not last long. God had given us too much grace, mercy, and discernment for us to ever dispose our gifts or use them for all the wrong reasons. On personal experience, early on I had explored almost every genre (except for country). During this stage of life, with little experience, my primary duty as a musician was to be eclectic in my musicality. As a songwriter, and to be transparent, my writing made little to no sense. I had a lot of passion and curiosity but little to no experience. My main focus was dance music starting out not because it was popular at the time, but because it was something I enjoyed. I had some regard for the lyrics I wrote but admittedly not as much as I should have had. Most of the lyrics were love songs and songs about going to dances and having a good time. As embarrassing as I was looking back at this, I cannot, in any means, justify it. It is all part of the creative process and comes with learning, unlearning, and relearning. It is natural in life for people to not really have consideration for those types of things (lyrics) as children. Learning from this, I can honestly and personally say, the music one listens to, just like content as a whole, reflects the values of that person. It is equally important to enjoy yourself and not lose your childlike wonder in the journey of life. That does not mean to engage in things that turn out to be harmful just because your peers are. I'm extremely grateful that I grew up not developing urges to resort to habits such as smoking, drinking, or worse. I have heard certain drugs boost creativity though I am not entirely sure. I am all for enhancers of creativity but if it puts your health and your faith on the line, then it is simply not worth it. From experience, the best type of music in the form of a message from

God and is poured out from the heart and soul of the performer or messenger in this case. This type of music contains truth, passion, either intensity or restraint, uncompromising musicality, and power. Power expands beyond the vocal range and pertains to the effects it has on the listener.

As a teenager, I was able to produce from a more critical standpoint and write about what may have occurred in my life and topics that I tend to passionate about. These themes included social injustice, girls I had an interest in, poverty, greed, racism, God's glory, perseverance, and many more. Whenever I connect with music, great music, I feel connected and reconnected to God. We have a tendency to connect with some of the wrong things in life and when we do, we do not feel as close to Him as we would like to. I apply this greatly to music. When I involve myself in music that promotes an unholy way of living, I find myself unable to connect with it, and if, God forbid, I ever did, it would probably feel forced just like it did the first few years of being a teenager. I may have been expanding my musical horizons, and I may have been doing what I've been called to do but the question was: Was I doing it the way it is intended? Most likely no. To receive a true transformation that started from the inside out, I needed to ask God if what I was being exposed to came from Him. If it did not, I had to rely fully on Him to completely remove it from my life and only He is capable of doing so.

Currently, I listen to mostly gospel/Messianic, jazz, classical, some R& B, and most recently, country. In the process of creating a new musical composition, I tend to look beyond these genres a bit and incorporate global types of music such as Latin and Arabic. I will continue to see what else God has in store for Drew and I in music. My journey as a writer, though much shorter, included a lot of personal and spiritual growth and transformation. I have only been writing things outside of music consistently for the last five years. During high school, I developed an interest in poetry. A lot of the inspiration for my poetry stems from some of the problems in the world, my mood whenever I started writing, particular books in the Bible, and experiences not just of my own but from others. In terms of personal figures, they included Amiri Baraka,

Maya Angelou, Lauryn Hill, and Pablo Neruda. I wrote with the intent to relate to the events of others. Over the years, I have delved into many styles of writing in addition to poetry including essays and business plans. One of the ways of becoming a great writer is writing what scares you, for it is part of the process of being uncomfortable. God does not expect us to remain complacent and comfortable in our lives, which is why we are in trials and tribulations in the process of something greater. There are plenty of times when I wrote what it is that I intended to write and ended up throwing it away after one mistake. No matter how little the mistake may have seemed, it did not sit well with me and I chose to restart. The reason I tend to not maintain works with mistakes is because prior to starting, God has given me a vision of the completed project, and I do not want to cease until I attain it the way it is intended. This was a lesson of humility. When I stopped wanting to pursue works because of personal gain or having concern for what people may say and instead realigned my focus with spiritual and eternal results and what God had in store, I was able to truly focus and my confidence boosted. Writing has given me a lot of benefits that I never expected. I had become more confident in who I am and in who God made me to be.

Because of it, it has allowed me to publish my first book in November 2015, Joys & Pains: Words From The Soul, which consists of poetry. Following this was Ascension: The Journey Continues in 2016. Year by year, it had improved through experience after experience. That is what life does for us. We all develop a story to share in any way we possibly can. I would say one of the biggest elements that has served as a catalyst in my creative journey was a sense of sensitivity and empathy. I admittedly have a sensitive heart, for better and sometimes for worse. Regardless, that sensitivity has allowed me to be who I authentically am in Christ. In a cruel world, there are ups and downs to having a sensitive heart, but the more you focus on the ups, God will resolve the downs for they are not compared to what He is able to provide to you. The more we are able to understand the emotions and feelings of others instead of just ourselves, the more we will be able to contribute in setting a better example. Sensitivity is one of the biggest blessings God has blessed me with. I never have to blend in with certain environments and behaviors because of it. It is a sign of courage. Some say it is a sign of weakness, but I beg to differ. It is a sign of everlasting strength and Godfidence that the world can never try to break.

Endnote by Jeffrey Hayzlett

Creativity has many forms. We often associate the word creativity with its output or expression: art, music, acting or writing. My wife and daughter are both very talented musicians and painters. I myself have a large collection of art, my favorites being Native American painters like JoAnne Bird and Jim Nelson. Put creativity and business together in the same sentence and they seem like a bit of an oddly-matched set. Like Bernadette Peters marrying Warren Buffett. Our traditional sense of business -- the suit-and-tie-world of mergers and acquisitions, Wall Street, and expansive board rooms – is a far cry from the free-flowing, inspirational, paintbrushes and the Broadway stage-like ideation that is creativity. But if you think for one second creativity has no place in your business, you are dead WRONG. Creativity is a key component of SUCCESS, of WINNING. And who doesn't want to win? I know I do! Let me explain. In order to be successful, you need to be what I call a "change agent." Change agents are the employees, leaders, even the janitor in your company who takes proactive, even risky, action to create, facilitate and even force change. A couple weeks into leading the marketing team at Kodak, I arrived at a meeting early, removed the clock from the wall and moved the time a few minutes. I sat back down and waited for my team. As they sat down and settled in, a couple of them looked at the clock, then their phones or watches and commented that the time was incorrect. "We really should have that fixed," said one. "Maybe someone should call maintenance," said another. This went on for days, then WEEKS. Then one day, after the "we should and maybe someone" conversation happened again, a woman on my team stood up, pushed her chair over to the wall, CLIMBED on the chair in her heels and skirt, took down the clock and CHANGED it. They all had the ability to take action, but not one of them did until the shortest person in the room decided to make it happen, to think outside the box and affect change. Creativity can be as simple as finding a solution to fix the time on a boardroom clock. Change agents are the ones who use their creativity to find solutions and make it happen. They refuse to compromise on creativity when they believe it's the right thing to do. Creativity is as simple as challenging a procedural hurdle. That's not to say that you shouldn't start by trying to follow procedure most of the time. You can compromise and slow things down, or just do what you think is the right thing, the most effective thing. Creativity is the best way to change the old way of doing things, to find new ways to do the right thing. Don't take the path of least resistance.

As a leader, an entrepreneur, a student, an employee, you have the opportunity to use creativity every day. Jordan's book offers real-life experience, actionable insights and ways to facilitate your creativity in business and in life. So pop on your favorite piece of music, sit in view one of your favorite painting and start reading. This book will help you become an agent of change.

-Jeffrey Hayzlett – Chairman of the C-Suite Network

Recommendations

For more creative inspiration, I highly recommend the following books to read:

Originals-Adam Grant

Teach Like a Pirate- Dave Burgess

Creative Confidence-Tom Kelley/ David Kelley

The War of Art-Steven Pressfield

The Artist's Way-Julia Camero

The Creative Curve- Allen Gannett

Acknowledgments

Your love and support for those reading is highly appreciated, valued and respected. This would not be possible without the grace of my Father in heaven and what/who He's allowed to cross my path and impact my life in a positive way. All glory goes to God and huge, infinite thanks and blessings to the following: My parents, Hiram Thomas and Le'ta Arnold, my twin, Drew Thomas, Eddie Mae Thomas, Karon Thomas, Sheryl Thomas, Stephanie Thomas (Rest in Peace), Edgar Thomas, Renee Thomas, Nicole Thomas, Ericka Dorsey, Latanya Jones, Nia Norwood, Savanna Morgan, Anthony Watts, James McGillberry, Daisia Lewis, Melissa Cadena, Ximenna Patten, Dave Koz, Pete Fotia, Bill Mulvehill, Cary Willborn, Chris Wenger, Doug Bailey, Sam Chand, Diego Mesa, Ty Tyler, Jesse Felix, David Janosky, Rashad Khawaja, Tamara Holder, Brandon Landrum, Cassandra Butcher, Evelyn Knox, Sefo Tomu, Muhammad Khan, Damarea Parker, Nicholas Jenkins, Prince Ogidikpe, Devonte Holston, Anthony Roberson, Alex Avila, Shaquel McCoy, Chris Bell, Cortney Polk, Monica Falconer, Nina Calub, Daiquan N'Kere, Leo Mullarky, Keith Rivas, Simba Peresuh, Sesedzayi Peresuh, Charles Seager, Bradley Hampton, Matthew Brady, Robert Knop, Susie Pryor, Mike Stull, Alfonso Anaya, Jose Ortiz, Musa Suliman, David P. Perlmutter, Jeffrey Hayzlett, Bruce Van Horn, Skip Prichard, Don Repenning, Matt Crane, Jim Beach, Cherie Aimee, Cel

Jonas Martinez, Greg Walker, Mark Minard, Shane De Garay, Frank Sagasta, Noel Walsh, Scott Nowlin, Joel Buhr, Joel Boggess, Vick Tipnes, Ken Rochon, John Cordray, John Cerrone, Peter Nez, Cherie Aimee, Anthony Conklin, Matt Maddix, Caleb Maddix, Bruno Coelho, Desiree Lee, Ruby Jackson, Morgan J. Ingram, Tyler Redman, Sean Wyman, Bill Wooditch, Rick Lawson, Mark Schaefer, Ted Rubin, John Sparks, Marvin LeBlanc, Jeffrey Shaw, Richard Trevino II, Josiah Ojeda, Tim Laskis, Walter Sims, Jacques Pedro Grooms, Jeremy Murphy, Sean Douglas, and many other amazing individuals.

www.ingramcontent.com/pod-product-compliance
Lightning Source LLC
Chambersburg PA
CBHW070232210526
45168CB00020B/2036